VICTORIA JUSTICE

Shine On!

By Riley Brooks

SCHOLASTIC INC.
New York Toronto London Auckland
Sydney Mexico City New Delhi Hong Kong

Photo Credits:
Front cover: Heart with string Copyright Madlen/ shutterstock.
Masking tape Copyright Steve Collender/shutterstock portrait Associated Press.
Blue background Copyright loriklaszlo/shutterstock.
Pg 1 Portrait: Associated Press. Pg 1 Red heart: Luciana Bueno/SHUTTERSTOCK.
Pg 1 Masking tape: Steve Collender/shutterstock. Pg 1 Picture frame: samantha grandy/shutterstock.
Pg 1 Blue background: loriklaszlo /shutterstock. Pg 2: Merkushev Vasiliy /shutterstock. Pg 4: Getty Images. Pg 6: FilmMagic/gettyimages. Pg 9: Getty Images. Pg 10: Wire Image/Gettyimages.
Pg 11: Getty Images. Pg 13: Wire Image/Gettyimages. Pg 14: Wire Image/Gettyimages.
Pg 17: Gettyimages. Pg 18: Associated Press. Pg 20: Gettyimages. Pg 23: Associated Press.
Pg 24: 2010 Getty Images. Pg 26: Associated Press Pg 27: FilmMagic/gettyimages. Pg 28: Wire Image/ Gettyimages. Pg 30: 2010 Getty Images. Pg 31: Associated Press.
Pg 33: Associated Press. Pg 34: 2011 Christopher Polk/KCA2011.
Pg 36: Associated Press. Pg 38: 2010 Getty Images. Pg 41: 2010 Getty Images.
Pg 42: Associated Press. Pg 45: Associated Press. Pg 47: 2011 Getty Images.
Pg 48: Associated Press. **Back cover:** 2011 Christopher Polk/KCA2011/ gettyimages.
Red heart Copyright Luciana Bueno /SHUTTERSTOCK.

ISBN 978-0-545-41565-1

12 11 10 9 8 7 6 5 4 3 2 1 12 13 14 15 16/0

Printed in the U.S.A. 40
First printing, January 2012

TABLE OF CONTENTS

INTRODUCTION

Have you ever wondered what it would be like to be the star of your very own show on Nickelodeon? See your face up on the big screen? Record albums and shoot music videos? It would be a total victory, right?

Well, Victoria Justice has pretty much won the superstar lottery. These days, Victoria is starring in one of the hottest shows on Nickelodeon, promoting her debut album and the soundtrack album for her hit show *Victorious*, and shooting several movies. But before she was a rising star, Victoria was just a regular girl growing up in Florida.

CHAPTER 1
LITTLE STAR

Victoria Dawn Justice was born on February 19, 1993, in Hollywood, Florida, to proud parents Zack and Serene. Since she grew up in Hollywood, it's no surprise that Victoria was destined for stardom in Hollywood, California! As she got older, her mom signed her up for dance lessons, and it soon became clear that Victoria was a natural performer. She was the star of her class in tap, ballet, and jazz dance!

When Victoria was three, she became a big sister to Madison Justice. Victoria's parents got divorced a few years later and her dad moved to South Carolina. Victoria really missed seeing her dad every day, but they keep in touch with lots of calls and visits.

Eventually, Victoria's mom married a great guy named Mark Reed. Victoria and her sister were always performing for their mom and her new husband, as Victoria explained to *Scholastic Magazine*: "I just liked being funny and entertaining people. I was always putting on shows with my friends and my sister."

Soon, Victoria realized that she wanted to do more than just dance. "I was eight years old, and was watching some kid on a commercial when I thought, *I want to be on TV*," Victoria explained to *Scholastic Magazine*. It was pretty clear to Victoria that she could be a star, so she begged her mom to help her. Luckily, Victoria's mom really believed in her daughter and knew just how talented she was! She took Victoria to a talent agent in nearby Miami, Florida, and before she knew it, Victoria was going to auditions all over the state.

CHAPTER 2
MODEL BEHAVIOR

Victoria took the entertainment industry in Miami by storm. With her shiny dark hair, big brown eyes, and dazzling smile, she was exactly what casting agents were looking for. And it didn't hurt that she could sing and dance like a pro as well! She modeled for fashionable brands like Gap and Guess.

Trips into Miami for modeling were more than just work—they were also fun bonding time for Victoria and her mom. "I have great memories of modeling on the beach, and then when I was done, my mom and I would go have dinner somewhere. It was great!" Victoria explained to *Scholastic Magazine.*

While Victoria looked beautiful in pictures, she was eager to show off her acting skills as well. And the people she auditioned for recognized her star power right away. Victoria booked a part on

her very first audition, as she explained to JustJaredJr.com: "My very first commercial was for Ovaltine, and I was so excited when I got that job . . . I felt like a star after I did that . . ."

Since that first ad, Victoria has done about thirty other commercials. Some of them were local spots based in Florida, but a lot of them aired nationally, like ones for Peanut Butter Toast Crunch and Mervyn's stores.

You could have seen Victoria on TV before she was a big star if you were watching carefully!

CHAPTER 3
SHOWBIZ SUMMERS

By 2003 Victoria was ready to try some bigger projects—like television shows and movies. So that summer, Victoria headed to Hollywood, California, with her mom and sister, to go to some big auditions.

It only took three weeks for Victoria to book her first role: guest-starring on an episode of the hit show *Gilmore Girls*. It was a Halloween episode so Victoria was dressed as a Hobbit for three solid days. It was over one hundred degrees outside and most kids would have been miserable—but not Victoria! Encouraged by her success, Victoria went on to book roles in two independent films—*Fallacy* and *When Do We Eat?*

Victoria spent the school year back in Florida

and continued modeling and acting in commercials. She landed a big ad campaign for the clothing brand Ralph Lauren that winter, and went back to Los Angeles the next summer, ready to try again. Within a few weeks, she booked a role in a national commercial for America Online and a role in an independent film called *My Purple Fur Coat*.

But Victoria's biggest audition of the summer was for the prestigious Millikan Middle School and Performing Arts Magnet in California. When she was accepted, her family decided to make the big move from Hollywood, Florida, to Hollywood, California, permanently.

CHAPTER 4
STARDOM 101

After the move, Victoria got right to work. She quickly booked a part guest-starring on *The Suite Life of Zack and Cody*, a hit show on Disney starring Dylan and Cole Sprouse. Victoria was especially excited about working with the super cute twin brothers! She also filmed

several independent movies—*The Garden, The Unknown*, and a Christmas-themed made-for-TV movie called *Silver Bells*.

Victoria loved working on such a large variety of projects. Plus, she got the chance to take acting and singing lessons from professionals. "I loved the fact that when it came to acting, any kind of training you were interested in was available here—from improv to musical theater and everything in between. For TV and film, this is where it all happens," Victoria explained to *Scholastic Magazine*.

All of Victoria's hard work paid off when she landed the role of "Lola" on the hit Nickelodeon show *Zoey 101* in 2005. Victoria was thrilled! Lola was Zoey's new roommate with a flair for drama—just like Victoria! "Lola is an aspiring actress who wants to win an Oscar by age nineteen. She has a really colorful, straight-out-of-*Vogue* fashion style that's reflected in her

clothes and hairstyles. You get the feeling that she's very confident and focused on her goal," Victoria explained to *Scholastic Magazine*.

Working on *Zoey 101* was a great experience for Victoria. She fit right in and made friends quickly. Not only that, she and the rest of the cast won two Young Artist Awards for Best Young Ensemble Performance in a TV Series (Comedy or Drama) in 2007 and 2008.

Being a series regular was a totally different experience for Victoria. She was used to doing projects that wrapped up after a few weeks, but the *Zoey* cast filmed all summer long for three years. It gave Victoria a chance to really dig into her character and create some awesome friendships.

Her co-stars, including Erin Sanders and Alexa Nikolas, were all around her age and they enjoyed hanging out when they weren't filming. It definitely didn't hurt that several of her

co-stars, like Matt Underwood, Christopher Massey, and Sean Flynn, were super cute boys! Victoria was really disappointed when *Zoey 101* came to an end in 2008, but she was excited for what the future might hold for her.

The

CHAPTER 5
VICTORY!

Luckily, Victoria didn't have to look far for her next big part—it actually came to her from Dan Schneider, the creator of *Zoey 101*. "When the show, [*Zoey 101*], was almost over, Dan had approached my mom about writing a show for me. I will never forget it," Victoria told *Glitter Magazine*. Dan Schneider is the creator of tons of teen shows, including *Zoey 101*, *Drake &*

Josh and *iCarly*, and it meant a lot to Victoria that he believed in her.

Dan really wanted to feature her amazing singing and dancing skills in addition to her acting. So they decided to base her new show on her real-life experiences at a performing arts school. "I was in a musical theater program from sixth to eighth grade in school, so it's very close to my own life. The kids I was surrounded by were artsy and talented just like my castmates," Victoria explained to Popeater.com.

Victorious premiered on March 27, 2010, and fans loved it. Victoria plays the role of "Tori Vega," an average girl who gets accepted into Hollywood Arts, a performing arts high school, along with her older sister. Tori gets caught up in lots of wacky situations and does plenty of singing and dancing on the show.

But it isn't Victoria alone on set. She has some great co-stars! She loves going shopping

with Elizabeth Gillies, snarky mean girl "Jade"; Ariana Grande, ditzy and sweet "Cat"; and Daniella Monet, Tori's older sister "Trina." Of course, Victoria always has a blast hanging out with cute co-stars Leon Thomas II, who plays songwriter "Andre"; Matt Bennett, who stars as the nerdy ventriloquist "Robbie"; and Avan Jogia, who plays the friendly and handsome "Beck."

Victoria loves her on-screen buds and they all hang out off the set as well, as she told *Glitter Magazine*: "We have an amazing cast. They're

all very talented in their own way. We have a lot of fun on set in between scenes. There's a lot of singing and playing instruments, because most of us are very musical."

Working on *Victorious* has been a dream come true for Victoria. It has allowed her to showcase for her fans her singing (including filming a few music videos for the show); it has made her a household name around the world; and it has opened up a lot of new opportunities for Victoria.

CHAPTER 6
MADE FOR TV

Before *Victorious* began filming, Victoria was cast as mean girl "Tammi" in *Spectacular!*, a made-for-television movie on Nickelodeon. Nick was excited to show off their new star, and the movie gave Victoria a chance to introduce to fans her singing and dancing skills. "There are a lot of cool musical performances. The songs are so

catchy and great!" Victoria gushed to *CosmoGirl*.

She costarred alongside Nolan Gerard Funk, Simon Curtis, Tammin Sursok, and Greg Germann, and had a great time filming with them. Her favorite scene to film was "probably the finale number, 'On the Wings of a Dream,' because the song was cool and because it was the finale. We all worked really, really extra hard on that number," Victoria told JustJaredJr.com. The movie looked fantastic when it was finished and had fans dancing and singing along in their living rooms when it premiered.

Victoria's performance in *Spectacular!* was such a hit that Nickelodeon signed her on for another made-for-TV movie called *The Boy Who Cried Werewolf* in 2010. Victoria played the lead role of "Jordan," a nerdy girl. She and her struggling family go to Wolfsburg, Romania, when they discover they've inherited their great-uncle Dragomir Vukovic's castle. While there,

Jordan turns into a werewolf and ends up fighting vampires.

Victoria loved working with the special effects. "It's been so much fun," Victoria told *J-14*. "I played around with physical comedy

and improv, and I got to do so much with the character. She really grows throughout the movie . . . It's a really great character arc and it was a lot of fun to play her." Fans had just as much fun with the movie as Victoria did and loved seeing her try something new.

But Victoria didn't just work on movies during her downtime, she also guest-starred on TV shows and did a little modeling. Victoria shot a special print campaign for the fifteenth anniversary of those famous milk mustache ads! "It was so much fun and such an honor to be

chosen for the fifteenth anniversary campaign. I shot at the new 'Milk' studios in L.A., and we shot two different looks. One was for print ads and the other for school posters," Victoria told *Glitter Magazine.*

And back in the world of television, Victoria guest-starred on several Nickelodeon shows, including *True Jackson, V.P., The Naked Brothers Band, The Troop, The Penguins of Madagascar,* and several episodes of *iCarly*. Working with fellow Nick stars like Miranda Cosgrove and Keke Palmer was so much fun for Victoria and she's hoping to have them guest-star on *Victorious* in the future!

CHAPTER 7
SINGING SENSATION

Victoria has always loved singing, so she was pretty excited when part of her contract for *Victorious* included a record deal. She was eager to jump right into recording her debut album, but knew she had to take the time to get it right.

It was really important for Victoria that she write a lot of her own music, as she explained to Latina.com: "It's going to be different from what people expect me to do. The direction that we're going in is an edgy, more mature sound . . . I want to sing songs that are meaningful to me. That's why I want to write my own material, because when I perform it onstage, I want to be able to really connect to it."

Victoria worked with a lot of experienced songwriters to create the perfect songs for her album. She's been inspired by a lot of different styles of music, but knows for sure that most of her songs will have a pop feel.

Of course, fans of her show also raced out to buy the soundtrack for *Victorious* featuring Victoria singing as Tori Vega. *Victorious* fans were able to download singles from the show, including "Freak the Freak Out," "Shine On," "Beggin' on Your Knees," and "Best Friend's

Brother" before the album's release. And they definitely loved the super cool music videos for "Beggin' on Your Knees" and "Freak the Freak Out," which Victoria had a blast filming! "It was really amazing. It [the music video for 'Freak the Freak Out'] was shot, for the most part, in a warehouse space in downtown Los Angeles . . . The whole cast was there and it was like one big party. I loved the choreography and I love the song. It has such high energy that it'll make you want to get up and dance," Victoria told Popeater.com. The soundtrack for *Victorious* featured all of the music from the show, plus some great new songs written by Victoria!

With two albums out and singles climbing the charts, Victoria is really excited about her music career. She's hoping to go on tour soon—so look for Victoria at a concert venue near you!

CHAPTER 8
VICTORIA UNPLUGGED

Ever wondered what Victoria is like behind the scenes? Turns out she's just like any other teen girl. She loves going on shopping sprees with her little sister in vintage boutiques and in shops like Urban Outfitters and BCBG.

When she's not working, Victoria prefers to be with her family and friends. "I really like to just hang out at home, watch movies, go to improv shows with friends—just kind of take

it slow and hang out with people," Victoria told *Savvy Magazine.*

Victoria has a lot of friends who aren't in show business, and hanging out with them helps keep her grounded. Of course, she spends a lot of time with her actor buddies, like Miranda Cosgrove and Taylor Lautner, as well. And when she has any sort of problem, she turns to her mom to help her figure out what to do. "I ask my mom for advice on everything, from my hair to work-related stuff to what I should say to a boy," Victoria explained to *Family Circle.*

Victoria spends as much time as she can working with her favorite charity, Girl Up, to give back to her community. Girl Up is a foundation for the United Nations that helps underprivileged teen girls. Victoria is really passionate about helping other teens, and Girl Up was a natural fit for her, as she explained to *Zooey Magazine*: "I had been looking for a charity that I really

wanted to support, and this one seemed like a great fit. Also, the fact that I could be a part of helping launch a new charity with the United Nations was of interest to me, because it gives it credibility. The main thing that was important to me was the fact that it was girls helping other girls who weren't as fortunate." Giving back makes Victoria feel as beautiful inside as she is on the outside!

Of course, like any teen girl, Victoria spends plenty of time thinking about guys! She has been way too busy for dating, but that doesn't mean she'll stay single forever! Victoria isn't looking to her fellow models or actors to take her to the movies. She wants a guy who's as down-to-earth as she is, as she explained to *Seventeen* magazine: "Guys who are charismatic and fun-loving and sweet and generous are the ones I want to date. Good looks are secondary for me—it's just the icing on the cake."

CHAPTER 9
WHAT'S NEXT?

So what does the future hold for Nick's teen queen? Victoria has already had two hit shows, guest-starred in other shows, filmed over thirty commercials, and been in numerous ad campaigns and independent films. But she's just getting started!

Victoria will continue to film *Victorious* and work on her music career full-time. But she's also passionate about growing as an actress, so she is filming two movies set to release in 2012. The first is *Fun Size*, a hilarious Halloween flick about a sarcastic teenage girl who is forced to take her little brother trick-or-treating and loses him. It was a great fit for Victoria, especially since it will allow her to play a slightly edgier character than she ever has before.

The other film will be *The First Time*, a romantic comedy in which she will play the male lead's dream girl. "Ultimately, I would love to be able to have a successful music career and be able to choose projects I'm really passionate about—whether it's indie films or blockbuster studio films. Lately I've been reading a lot of scripts and looking for a great character. I'm really looking for something that grabs me . . . that when I read it, I know I have to have the role," Victoria explained to *Savvy Magazine*.

No matter what she's doing, from acting to dancing to modeling to singing, there is no doubt that Victoria will be victorious far into the future!

CHAPTER 10
JUST THE FACTS

Name: Victoria Dawn Justice

Birthday: February 19, 1993

Nickname: Vicky

Parents: Zack Justice, Serene Reed, and stepdad Mark Reed

Pets: dogs Sammy and Sophie

Siblings: younger sister Madison

Hometown: Hollywood, Florida

Current City: Hollywood, California

Favorite Celebrity: Oprah

Favorite Food: steak with a loaded baked potato

Hobbies: karaoke, watching movies, reading, and going swimming

Favorite Romantic Movies: *Sleepless in Seattle*, *When Harry Met Sally*, and *Jerry Maguire*

Favorite Color: turquoise

Favorite Band: the Beatles

FOX
THE 42ND NAACP IMAGE AWARDS
FOX
THE 42ND NAACP IMAGE AWARDS
FOX
FOX
THE 42ND NAACP IMAGE AWARDS
FOX
THE 42ND NAACP IMAGE AWARDS
FOX